Get to Work with Science and Technology

Master Blasters

Working with Explosives in Demolition and Construction

by Ruth Owen

Consultant:

Brent Blanchard
Implosion World.com

Ruby Tuesday Books

Published in 2017 by Ruby Tuesday Books Ltd.

Editor: Mark J. Sachner
Designers: Tammy West and Emma Randall
Production: John Lingham

Photo Credits:
Alamy: 5, 11 (bottom), 12 (bottom), 16 (top), 18, 19 (bottom), 20–21, 23, 29 (top); Creative Commons: 24–25; Getty Images: 8–9, 22; Press Association Images: 15; Ruby Tuesday Books: 26; Shutterstock: Cover, 4, 6–7, 10, 11 (top), 14 (bottom), 18 (top), 27, 28, 29 (bottom), 30; Wikipedia Public Domain: 13, 14 (top), 16 (bottom), 17.

Library of Congress Control Number: 2016907604

ISBN 978-1-910549-93-3

Printed and published in the United States of America

For further information including rights and permissions requests, please contact our Customer Service Department at 877-337-8577.

Contents

Call in the Blasters

A hurricane-damaged 30-story building must be **demolished**. It is too difficult and dangerous to take apart the structure piece by piece. All around the **condemned** tower are shops, hotels, and people's homes that must not be harmed.

This is the challenge. So what's the solution? It's time to call in the demolition experts known as blasters.

The 1515 Tower in West Palm Beach, Florida, crumples as 2,000 pounds (907 kg) of dynamite does its work.

It can take a team of blasters months to prepare a building for demolition. It takes less than 10 seconds for the building to be reduced to rubble!

Blasters are highly skilled **engineers** who rig a building with **dynamite**. The explosive **charges** are placed with absolute precision to ensure that a building collapses within a specific area. When the explosives are **detonated**, the building's framework must shatter. Then **gravity** does the rest!

The remains of the 1515 Tower

The World of Demolition

There are many reasons why a building is demolished. It might be unsafe because it's been damaged by fire or extreme weather. The ground where it stands may be needed for a new construction project. Sometimes old factory buildings are demolished when companies go out of business.

Most demolition is carried out by expert workers using excavators and other machines. Even tall buildings can be pulled apart by high-reach excavators.

Demolition site

High-reach excavator

Some high-reach excavators have a boom, or long arm, that can reach up to 200 feet (61 m).

Jaw-like tools are attached to an excavator's boom, or arm. These powerful tools can tear down walls, crush concrete, and cut through steel.

Sometimes, however, a building is too tall or too massive to be demolished by people and machines. In these cases, an explosive demolition is the only answer.

Demolition experts try to recycle metal, bricks, and other materials. Excavators scoop chunks of concrete and other debris into a rubble crusher. This material is crushed and can be used as part of the **foundation** for a new building.

Rubble crusher

Excavator

Crushed rubble

Debris from demolition

An Explosives Demolition

When blasters demolish a building, they place just the right amounts of explosives in exactly the right places to destroy parts of the building's structure. Once its structure is weakened, a building's weight and gravity bring it down.

The Central Police Station in Christchurch, New Zealand, is expertly brought down in May 2015. The building had been damaged by an earthquake.

Explosives engineers control which way a building falls by placing explosives in specific parts of the building. Then they detonate them in the right order. If a building needs to topple toward the north into an unused parking lot, they detonate explosives on the north side of the building first. Then the building's north side topples and pulls the rest of the building with it.

The 30-story Landmark Tower in Fort Worth, Texas, was imploded in March 2006.

A building may be surrounded on all four sides by streets, homes, and other structures. Then a difficult and risky operation called an **implosion** is carried out. The explosives are set up so that the building collapses straight down into its own **footprint**.

The Blast Plan

Once a team of blasters is hired to demolish a building, they must carefully plan the project. They begin by examining old **blueprints** of the building. These highly detailed plans show a building's structure and what it's made of.

The team visits the derelict building to assess its construction. How deep are the concrete columns that hold up each story? Could there be thick steel beams inside the columns?

Forget fashion! Life as a blaster means wearing protective clothing, such as a hard hat, steel-capped boots, or fluorescent overalls.

Blueprints are drawn by a building's designer, or architect. They show construction workers exactly how to put together the building.

Preparing a Blast Plan

Explosives on an upper floor will break up the building into smaller pieces. This makes life easier for the clean-up crew disposing of the rubble.

Supporting columns

To collapse the building, explosives may be placed on supporting columns on the lower floor.

An explosives engineer might use a computer program to create a 3D model of the building. Then the explosives are added to the model and the engineer runs a virtual test of the blast to see how the building will collapse.

Blasters may spend weeks in a dusty, dangerous old building making detailed notes. With no elevators in operation, this can mean climbing up and down cold, dark stairwells hundreds of times!

Once all the **data** is collected, the team designs a blast plan.

It's not just tall buildings that are demolished by explosives. Here, blasts are detonated to destroy the Wulihe Stadium in Shenyang, China.

Preparing the Blast

With a blast plan in place, the blasters get to work drilling thousands of holes in the sections of the building that will be blown up. Each hole is then packed with an explosive charge.

To blow up concrete, blasters usually use dynamite. To demolish parts of a building made of steel, an explosive called cyclotrimethylenetrinitramine is used. This explosive is also known as RDX (Research Development Formula). When RDX is ignited, it expands at 5 miles per second (8 km/s), slicing through thick steel.

Before the blasters start work, a destruction crew might weaken a structure so it gives way more easily. The crew removes inside walls and fractures concrete columns by smashing them with sledgehammers.

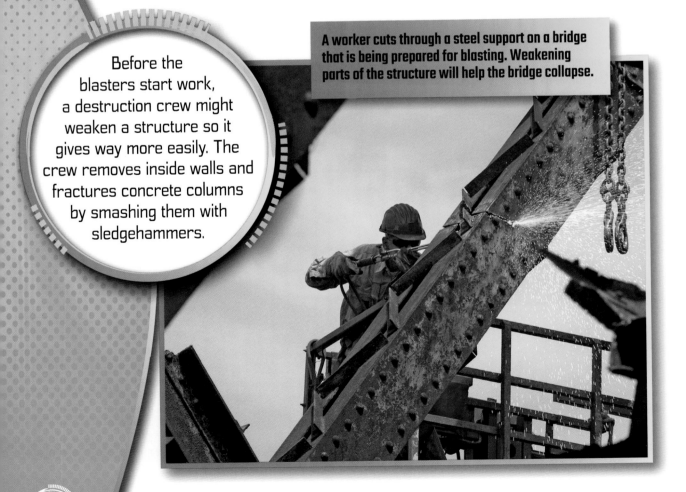

A worker cuts through a steel support on a bridge that is being prepared for blasting. Weakening parts of the structure will help the bridge collapse.

To ignite a charge, it must be connected to a **detonator** outside the building. This is done with a long cord called a detonating cord. The blasters lay miles of det-cord throughout the building, connecting all the explosive charges to the detonator.

Setting up the thousands of explosive charges inside a building may take a team of blasters several weeks, or even months.

An Explosive Charge

The detonating cord is a long cord connected to the detonator.

A traditional det-cord contains material that burns steadily. When the det-cord is lit, the flame travels along the cord and ignites the blasting cap.

Today, det-cords usually carry an electrical charge that ignites the blasting cap.

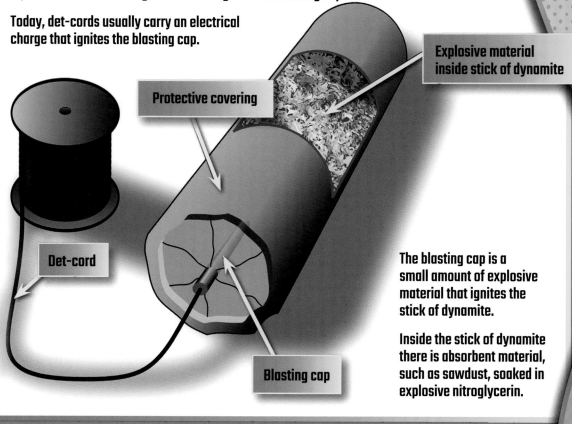

Protective covering

Explosive material inside stick of dynamite

Det-cord

Blasting cap

The blasting cap is a small amount of explosive material that ignites the stick of dynamite.

Inside the stick of dynamite there is absorbent material, such as sawdust, soaked in explosive nitroglycerin.

Precision and Safety

When all the explosives are in place, the building must be made safe. The crew wraps every column that will be blown up in chicken wire and thick plastic sheeting called geotextile fabric. As the column blows apart, these protective wrappings keep debris from being blasted out of the building. Flying chunks of concrete could cause damage to nearby buildings or even injure onlookers.

These concrete columns have been loaded with explosives and wrapped in geotextile fabric.

The yellow cord is the det-cord that will connect the charges to a detonator.

Attention to detail is essential when planning a blast.

The blasters' work must be absolutely precise. Every detail is checked again and again. If the explosives are placed incorrectly, the building might fall in the wrong direction, crushing neighboring buildings. If a mistake is made, the building might only partially fall. Then the explosives crew would be left with an unstable, potentially lethal structure that could collapse at any time.

Before the big day, an exclusion zone is set up around the blast site. Security guards might be hired to patrol the area. This ensures that no one, except the blasting crew, can get close to the building.

Geotextile fabric

Geotextile fabric

On the floors where blasting will take place, geotextile fabric is wrapped around the outside of the building.

Blast Day

It's the day of the blast. At a safe distance from the building, the blasting crew waits for the minutes to tick by. Sometimes a warning siren is sounded 10 minutes before the blast is scheduled. Then again at five minutes and one minute before blasting.

A detonator controller

Finally, the moment is here. The blaster takes hold of the detonator controller and the countdown begins. Five… four… three… two… one. Fire!

Bang! Bang! Bang! Like extreme firecrackers, the blasts echo around the building as each explosive charge detonates in exactly the right order.

The protective wrappings help contain any flying debris.

The building slides from view collapsing into a giant billowing cloud of dust.

A crew watches videos of a blast and carefully examines the site to make sure that every charge exploded. Any charges that did not detonate must be found and removed.

A building that may be decades old is gone in just a few seconds.

A Head for Heights

Some jobs require a blaster to have a head for extreme heights!

For decades, many power plants have generated electricity by burning coal. Today, some of these environmentally unfriendly coal-fired power plants are being decommissioned or shut down. When this happens, the blasters may be called in to demolish a power plant's giant **cooling towers**, high chimney stacks, and other structures.

In order to set up the explosives, the blasters may work inside the giant tower. They may also work from a cradle dangling on the outside of a tower.

A cradle on the outside of a power plant's cooling tower.

To ensure that the tower crumples in on itself, the blasting crew drills thousands of holes at precise locations high up the tower and at its base. Then the holes are packed with explosives.

In 2008, a team of blasters blew up the twin cooling towers at Tinsley Power Station in the UK. The team had to ensure that the towers did not fall toward the highway that ran alongside the towers.

A cooling tower imploding

The excavators move in to finish the demolition of one of the cooling towers at Tinsley Power Station.

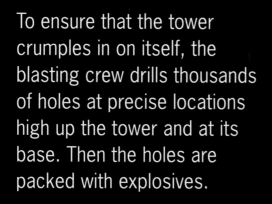

Highway

Precision Blasting

On September 26, 2015, two years of detailed planning and hard work came to an end with the dramatic demolition of Cockenzie Power Station's twin chimney stacks. The coal-fired power plant in Scotland had been in operation for 45 years. Now the plant was closed and the land would be **redeveloped**.

At 489 feet (149 m) high, each of the chimneys was taller than a 40-story building. A blast plan was devised to make the chimneys fall toward each other and impact 459 feet (140 m) above the ground. To achieve this, the blasting team drilled 1,500 holes in each chimney and packed them with explosives. The blasters' plan went without a hitch, and the chimneys crashed to the ground in a cloud of dust and rubble!

Chimney stack

People love to watch explosive demolitions. When Cockenzie Power Station was blasted, some people watched from their boats in the nearby bay. A local resident, Donald McCulloch, won a raffle to become a blaster for the day and get to push the "fire" button!

Cockenzie's turbine hall, where the electricity was once generated, was sent crashing to the ground just after the chimneys.

Blasting Tunnels

If you've ever ridden on a subway or traveled through a mountain tunnel, you've probably got explosives engineers to thank for your journey. Some explosives engineers use their skills to work on challenging tunneling projects, often deep underground.

To blast a tunnel through solid rock, engineers use a process called the "drill and blast" method. A machine called a drilling jumbo is used to drill a pattern of holes in the rock face. Then the holes are filled with explosives.

When the explosives are detonated, the rock face cracks, breaking up into rubble that can be hauled away.

Drilling jumbo

Rock face

On a tunneling project, an explosives engineer will work with rock scientists called geologists. A geologist gathers data on the rock's hardness and how its layers have formed. This data is used to create the blasting plan.

The angle, size, and spacing of the holes must be precise to suit the make-up of the rock.

Boxes of dynamite

Explosives engineers pack a rock face with dynamite.

Just as in demolition blasting, the placing of the explosives to blast a tunnel must be highly accurate. Get the blast wrong, and it could start a rockslide above ground or cause the tunnel to collapse. If the team is tunneling under a city, a mistake could damage buildings or roads on the surface.

Blasting Beneath a City

Deep below the bustling streets of New York City, explosives engineers are hard at work in a subterranean world. These engineers are working on the East Side Access project. They are building train tunnels, platform areas where people will catch trains, and shafts for elevators and escalators.

Each day, the blasters descend more than 10 stories beneath the city streets. Here, water drips from the rocky ceilings of the tunnels and enormous caverns. The dusty air is filled with the hum of heavy machinery.

This vast cavern was blasted from solid rock deep beneath Grand Central Terminal.

The explosives engineers and other workers who build tunnels beneath New York City are known as Sandhogs. Here, a crew is packing a rock face with explosives.

Using the drill and blast method, these engineers are blasting through rock that's more than 350 million years old. One day in the future, more than 160,000 people will travel through these tunnels every day.

Some of the tunneling for the East Side Access project has been carried out by blasting. A giant tunnel-boring machine has also been used.

Explosive charges detonating in a tunnel under New York City.

Blasting for Raw Materials

Some explosives experts work in mines. They blast rock to reach coal or obtain ores, which are rocks that contain metal. Others work in quarries, blasting rock from the ground to be used in construction.

A blast engineer at a quarry might need to design a blast plan that fragments a rock face, turning it into a giant heap of rubble. This broken rock is used as a base material beneath sidewalks, roads, and buildings. Crushed rock is also mixed with sand, cement, and water to make concrete.

Houses, apartment buildings, sidewalks, roads, school buildings, cars, planes, computers, coins, even soda cans…. Without the work of explosives engineers in mines and quarries, we would not have the raw materials to make all these things.

Blasting a Rock Face

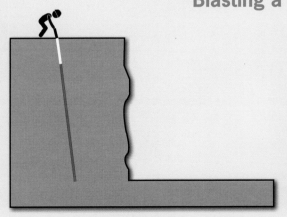

Holes are drilled and filled with explosives.

The explosives are detonated, shattering the rock.

An explosives engineer at a quarry might have to blast a house-sized, 40,000-pound (18,144-kg) block of granite from a rock face. Cutting machines are then used to cut the rock into smaller blocks. The granite might be used as blocks for building houses, pavement, or kitchen countertops.

This picture shows where blocks of granite have been removed from the rock face at a quarry.

Life's a Blast!

A blasting project involves day after day of painstaking preparation work. Then finally, the big day arrives. The tension is almost unbearable as the explosives detonate. A blaster knows instantly if she or he has gotten it right, or if something has gone wrong.

Boom! If all that's left is an enormous heap of debris, the blaster can feel relief and pride at a job well done. If something has not gone according to plan, the blaster must carefully assess what went wrong, and then use this information when planning future blasts.

Explosive demolition is an unusual and potentially dangerous career. But if you like the idea of combining detailed, meticulous engineering and science work with the high drama of explosions, blasting could just be the life for you!

The head blaster working on a demolition is sometimes known as the "Master Blaster." Experienced blasters who've demolished lots of buildings may also be given this title.

As the Wulihe Stadium collapses, a vast dust cloud rises from the structure.

The dust cloud caused by an explosive demolition looks dramatic, but it quickly settles. It is actually more neighborhood-friendly than a traditional demolition that may cause dust and noise for several months.

Q&A

What subjects should I study to become an explosives engineer?
In school, study math and science. In college, you might study engineering, construction, math, chemistry, or physics.

Can you learn blasting on the job?
Yes! Many blasters actually learn how to do this job by working for a demolition company. At first, your tasks might include carrying equipment, helping out in the office, or getting coffee. But work hard and take note of everything that the experienced engineers do, and you could get the chance to learn blasting and take part in demolitions.

Where do blasters work?
An experienced blaster might travel all over the world demolishing buildings and other structures. Demolition sites can be cold, wet, dirty places, though, so you must be tough to be a blaster.

Is working as a blaster dangerous?
Blasters work with highly dangerous explosives and often spend long periods of time in buildings that are very old or unsafe. Blasters take safety very seriously, though—their own, their co-workers, and the general public's. They follow lots of safety rules and never take risks!

Play Demolition Jenga!

If you've ever played Jenga, you'll know the object of the game is to build a tower of wooden blocks without causing it to fall over.

Demolition Jenga gives you a chance to think like a blaster and design a way to make the tower topple. Here's how to play with two players.

1. In this game, each player takes a turn controlling the tower and being the blaster. Begin by building a Jenga tower on a flat surface, as shown in the pictures.

2. The blaster's opponent must now say in which direction the tower should topple.

3. The blaster removes blocks from the tower one by one. The object is to weaken the structure so it topples in the right direction. The blaster must topple the tower by removing the fewest blocks possible, thinking carefully about the tower's weight and changing structure.

4. Once the tower topples, the blaster gets 10 points if it toppled in the correct direction. The blaster loses a point for every block removed from the tower. (The blaster's score may be a negative number.)

5. Now the opponent becomes the blaster and takes his or her turn. The winner is the player with the most points.

It sounds easy, but it's surprisingly difficult to topple a tower!

Glossary

blueprints (BLOO-printss)
Detailed technical drawings that show the design of a building, vehicle, or machine. Blueprints were originally printed on a blue background, which gave them their name.

charge (CHARJ)
A quantity of explosives (such as inside a stick of dynamite) that is connected to a detonating cord.

condemned (kuhn-DEMD)
In the case of a building, judged unfit or unsafe to be used. A building might be condemned by structural engineers who carefully examine its structure.

cooling tower (KOOL-ing TOU-ur)
A large chimney-like tower that is used to remove heat from a power plant or other type of factory.

data (DAY-tuh)
Information and facts, often in the form of numbers.

demolished (dee-MAH-lisht)
Taken apart or destroyed.

detonate (DET-uh-nate)
To cause something to explode.

detonator (DET-uh-nay-tur)
A control device connected to an explosive charge by a detonating cord. When fired, the detonator causes the charge to explode.

dynamite (DYE-nuh-mite)
A type of explosive made of absorbent material soaked in nitroglycerin. It is usually in the form of a stick, or tube.

engineer (en-juh-NIHR)
A person who uses math, science, and technology to design, build, repair, or demolish machines or structures.

footprint (FUT-print)
The amount of space on the ground that is covered by a building or other structure.

foundation (foun-DAY-shun)
The part of a building or other structure that connects it to the ground.

gravity (GRA-vuh-tee)
The force that causes objects to be pulled toward other objects. On Earth, we experience gravity pulling us, and everything around us, to the ground.

implosion (im-PLO-zhuhn)
A controlled blast that causes a building or other structure to collapse within its own footprint.

redeveloped (ree-di-VEL-uhpt)
Used for new construction projects.

Index

Read More

Beyer, Mark. *Demolition Experts: Life Blowing Things Up (Extreme Careers)*. New York: Rosen Publishing (2001).

Woolf, Alex. *Buildings (Design and Engineering for STEM)*. Mankato, MN: Heinemann-Raintree (2013).

Learn More Online

To learn more about blasters, go to:
www.rubytuesdaybooks.com/blasters